TRAVEL SIZE

?

TRUTH

OR

DARE

COLORING BOOK !

By Dani Kates

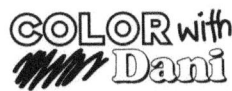

COLOR with
Dani

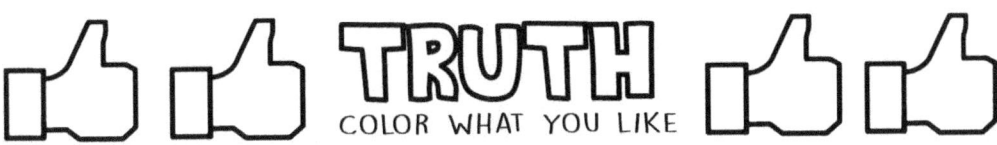

TRUTH
COLOR WHAT YOU LIKE

THIS OR THAT. COLOR ONE!

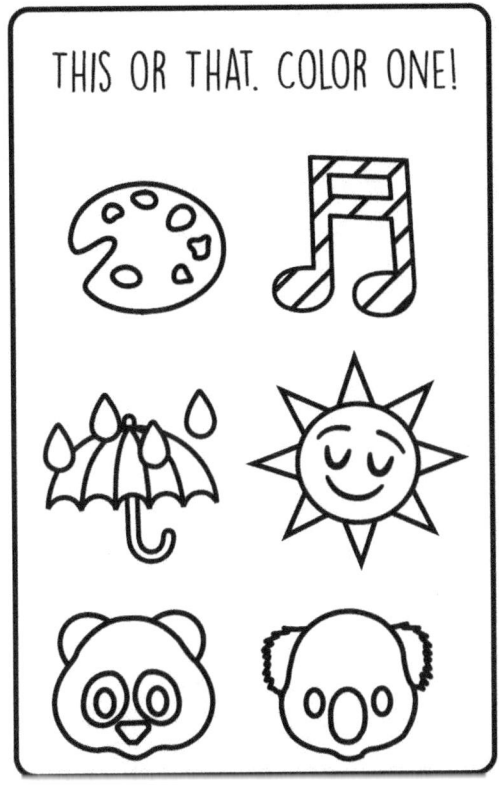

THIS OR THAT. COLOR ONE!

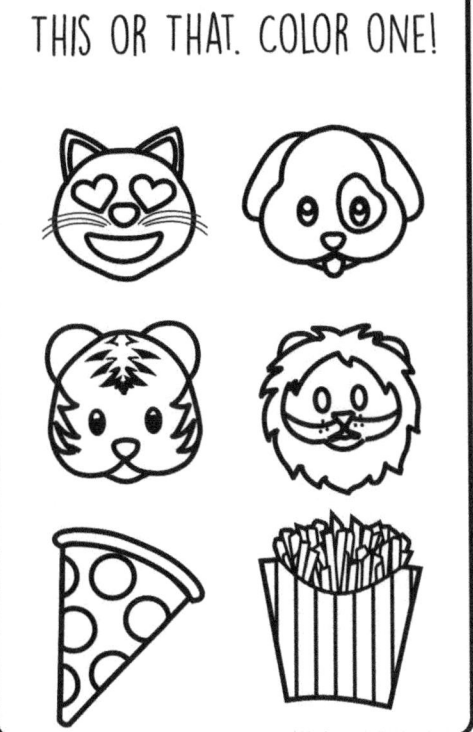

WHAT DO YOU LIKE TO EAT FOR BREAKFAST?

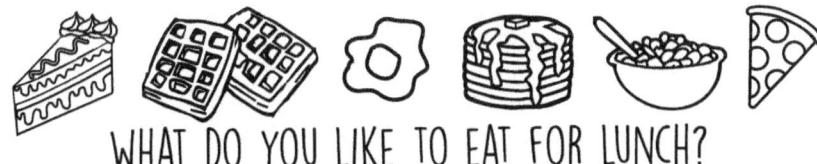

WHAT DO YOU LIKE TO EAT FOR LUNCH?

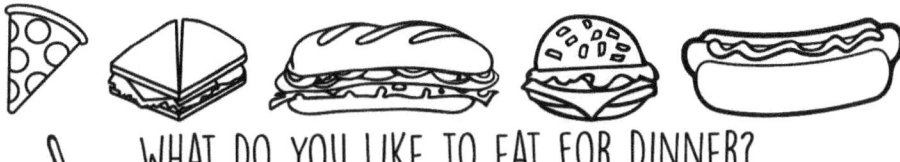

WHAT DO YOU LIKE TO EAT FOR DINNER?

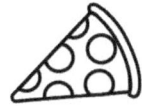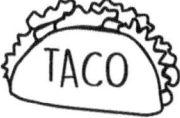

I DARE YOU TO...

COLOR THESE HANDS AND NAILS WITH YOUR <u>OTHER</u> HAND.

THAT MEANS IF YOU ARE A RIGHTY, USE YOUR LEFT HAND.
IF YOU ARE A LEFTY, USE YOUR RIGHT HAND!

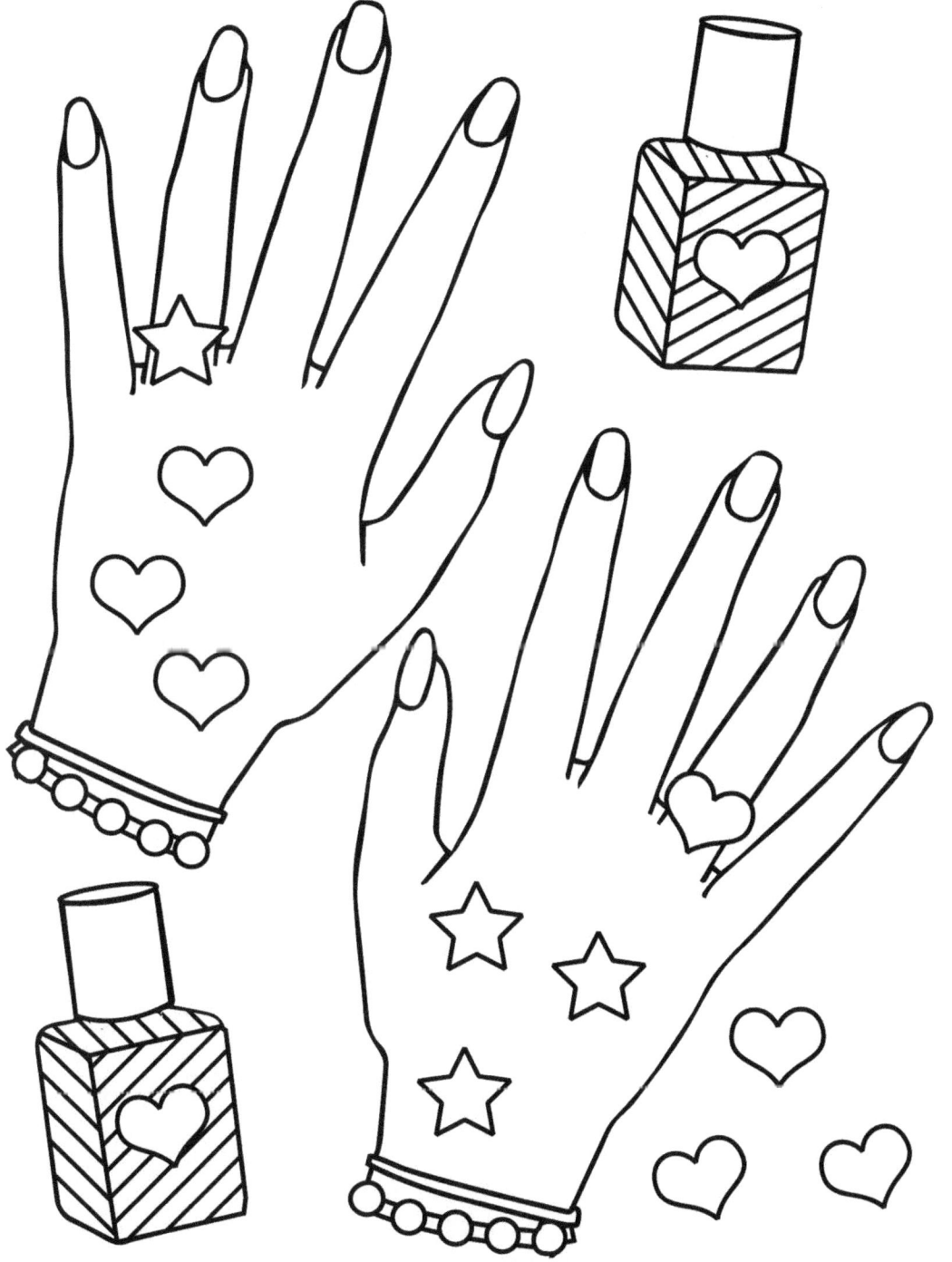

TRUTH

WOULD YOU RATHER EAT 5 SPIDERS OR KISS A SHARK?

Color your choice !

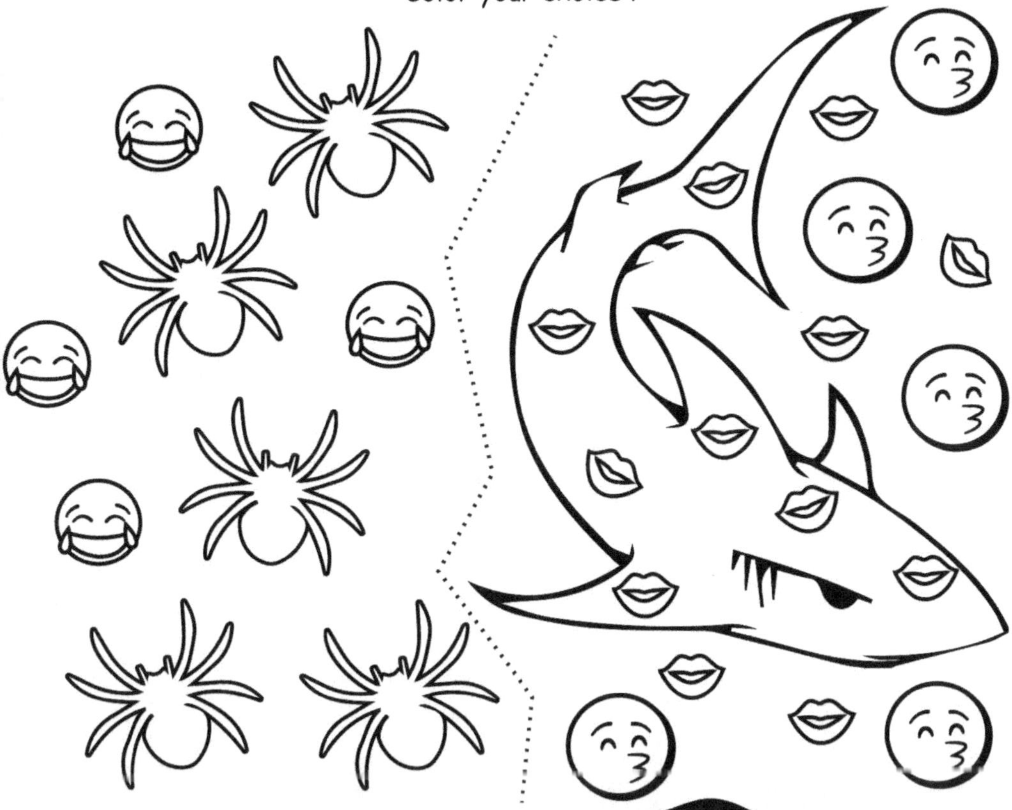

WHAT'S THE GROSSEST THING YOU EVER ATE?

_____

WHAT'S THE LAST THING IN THE WORLD YOU WOULD WANT TO EAT?

_____

THAT WAS GROSS. LET'S THINK OF SOMETHING LESS GROSS...PICK ONE

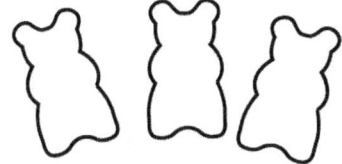   OR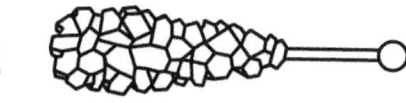

I DARE YOU TO...

COLOR ALL OF THESE HEARTS WITH YOUR EYES CLOSED!

START WITH YOUR EYES OPEN AND PUT YOUR FINGER IN THE MIDDLE OF THE CENTER HEART.
THEN CLOSE YOUR EYES, MOVE YOUR FINGER AWAY, AND START COLORING.
SEE IF YOU CAN GUESS WHERE THE OTHER HEARTS ARE!
NO PEEKING!

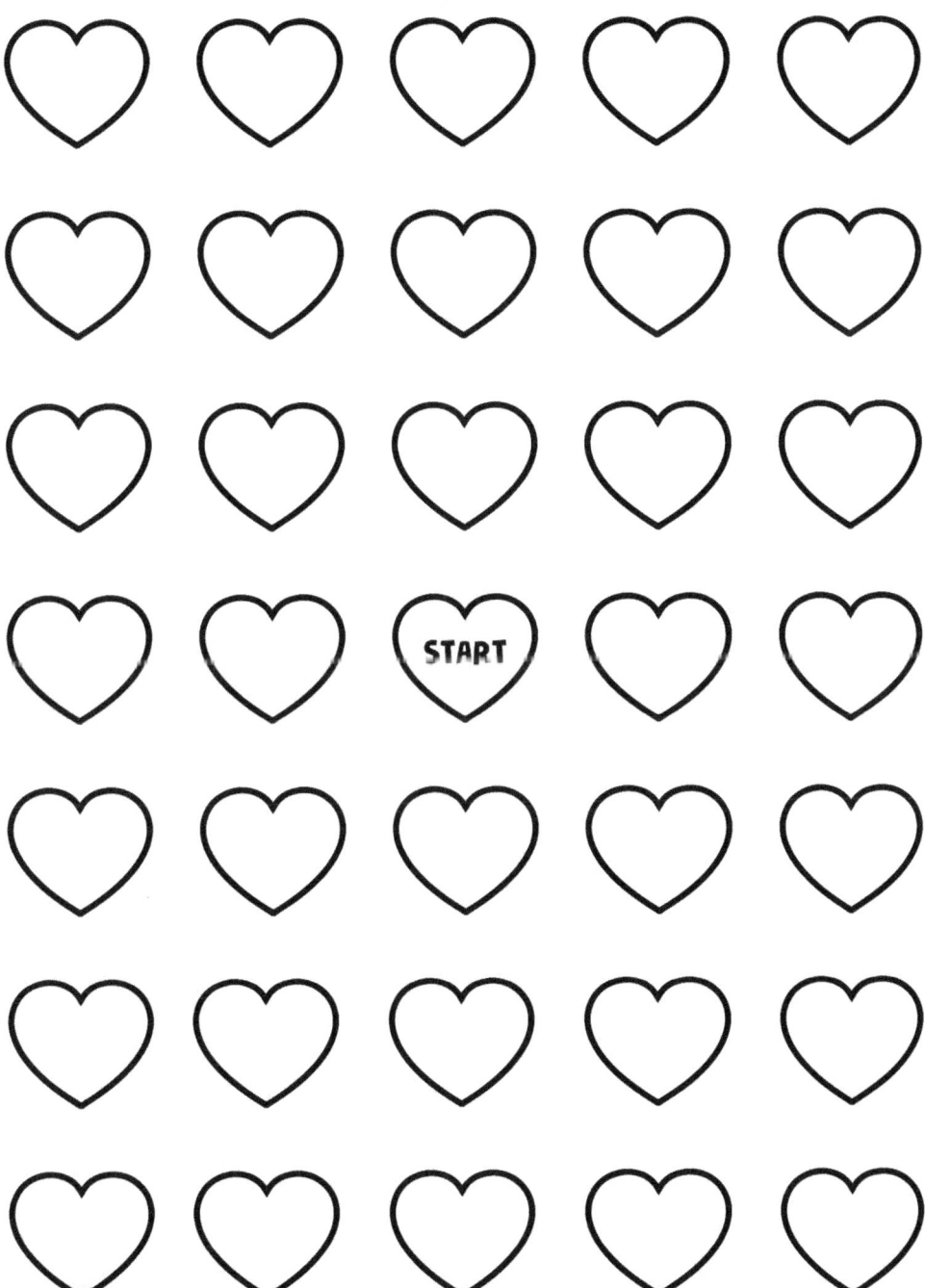

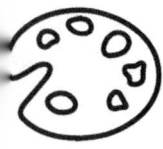 # TRUTH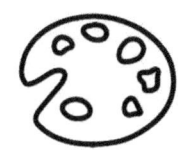

What colors do you love the most?

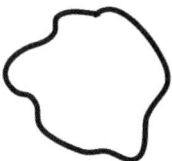 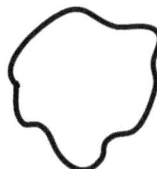 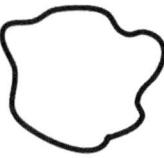 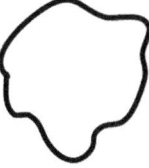

What colors do you NOT like?

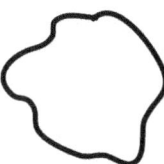 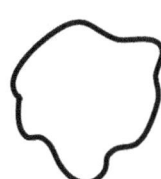 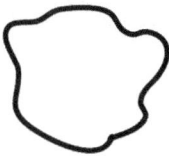 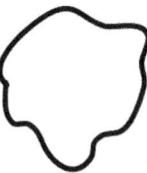

Color one rainbow with the colors you love and one with the colors you DON'T like !

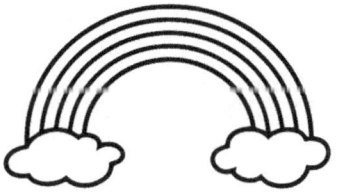 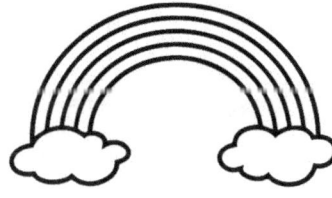

Favorite color for:

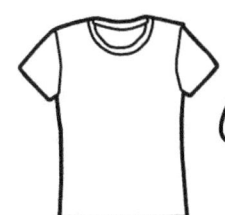 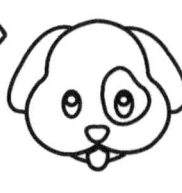 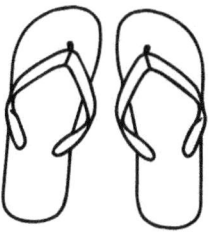 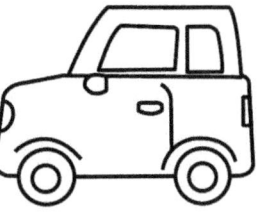

What do you like better stripes or polka dots?

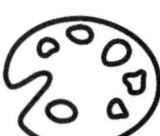 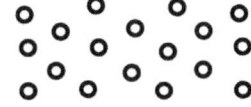 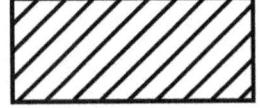 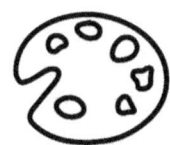

I DARE YOU TO...

COLOR THESE FLIP FLOPS WITH YOUR FEET!

OMG YES, REALLY! HOLD A CRAYON OR COLORED PENCIL BETWEEN YOUR BIG TOE & SECOND TOE AND START COLORING!!! THIS ONE IS NOT VERY EASY BUT IT IS VERYYY FUN !!

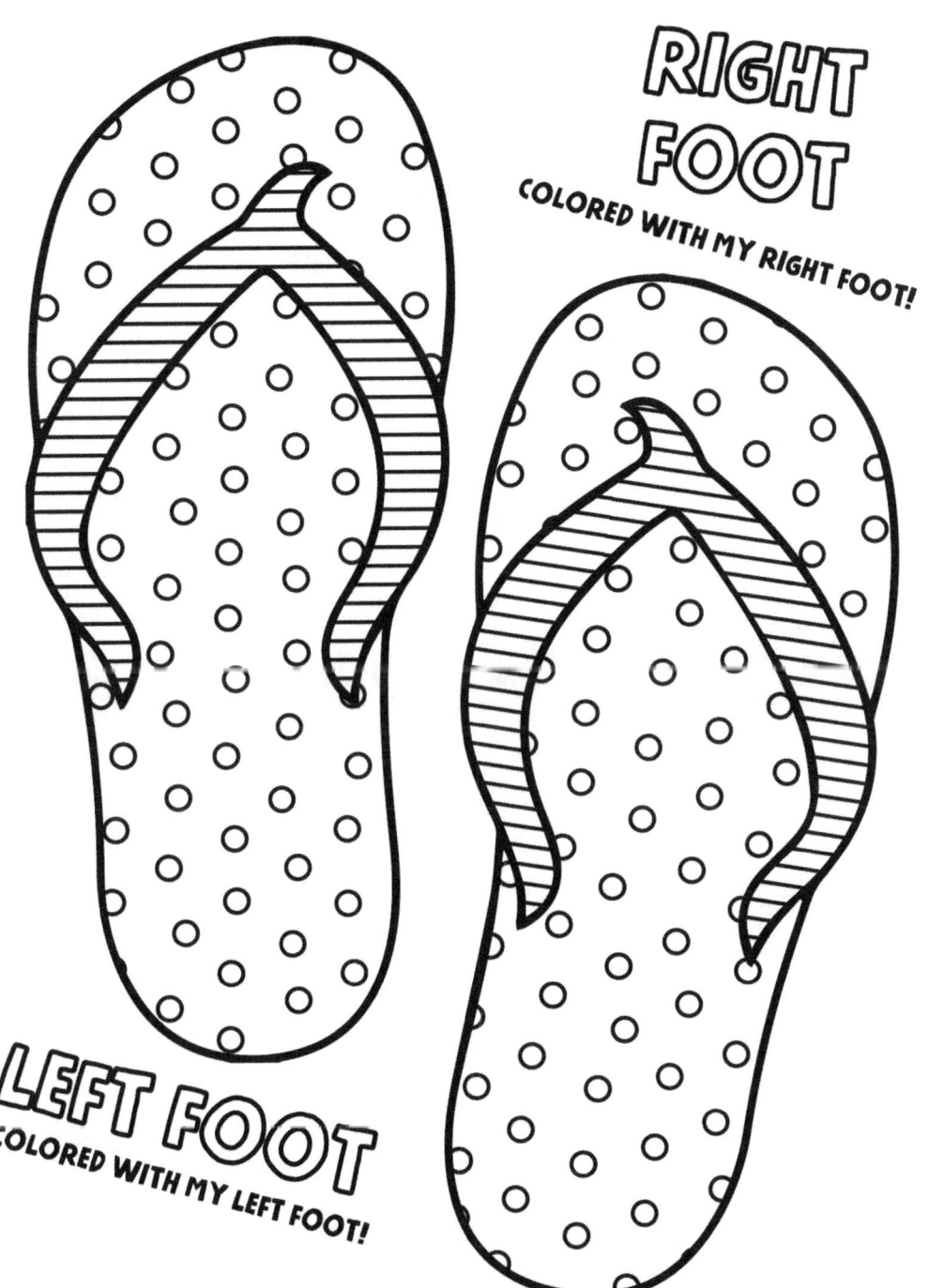

RIGHT FOOT
COLORED WITH MY RIGHT FOOT!

LEFT FOOT
COLORED WITH MY LEFT FOOT!

TRUTH

Would you rather be a princess or a mermaid?

Color your choice and draw or glue a picture of your face on it!

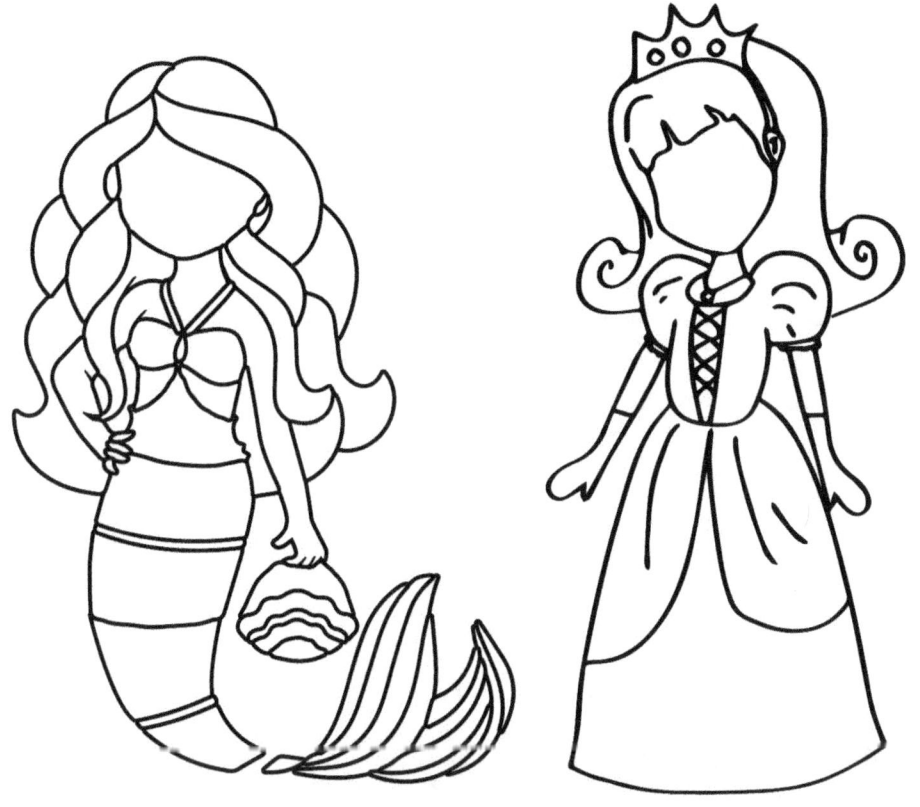

IF I COULD CHOOSE BETWEEN A PRINCESS AND A MERMAID

I WOULD BE A _____. I WOULD LIVE IN _____.

MY HAIR WOULD BE _____ AND I WOULD WEAR

_____ AND_____.

EVERYDAY I WOULD _____. MY FRIENDS WOULD BE

_____ AND _____.

MY FAVORITE THING ABOUT BEING A _____ WOULD BE

THAT I COULD _____ !

I DARE YOU TO...

TO COLOR WITH YOUR LEFT AND RIGHT HAND AT THE SAME TIME !
TURN THE BOOK SIDE WAYS. IT WILL BE EASIER THAT WAY!

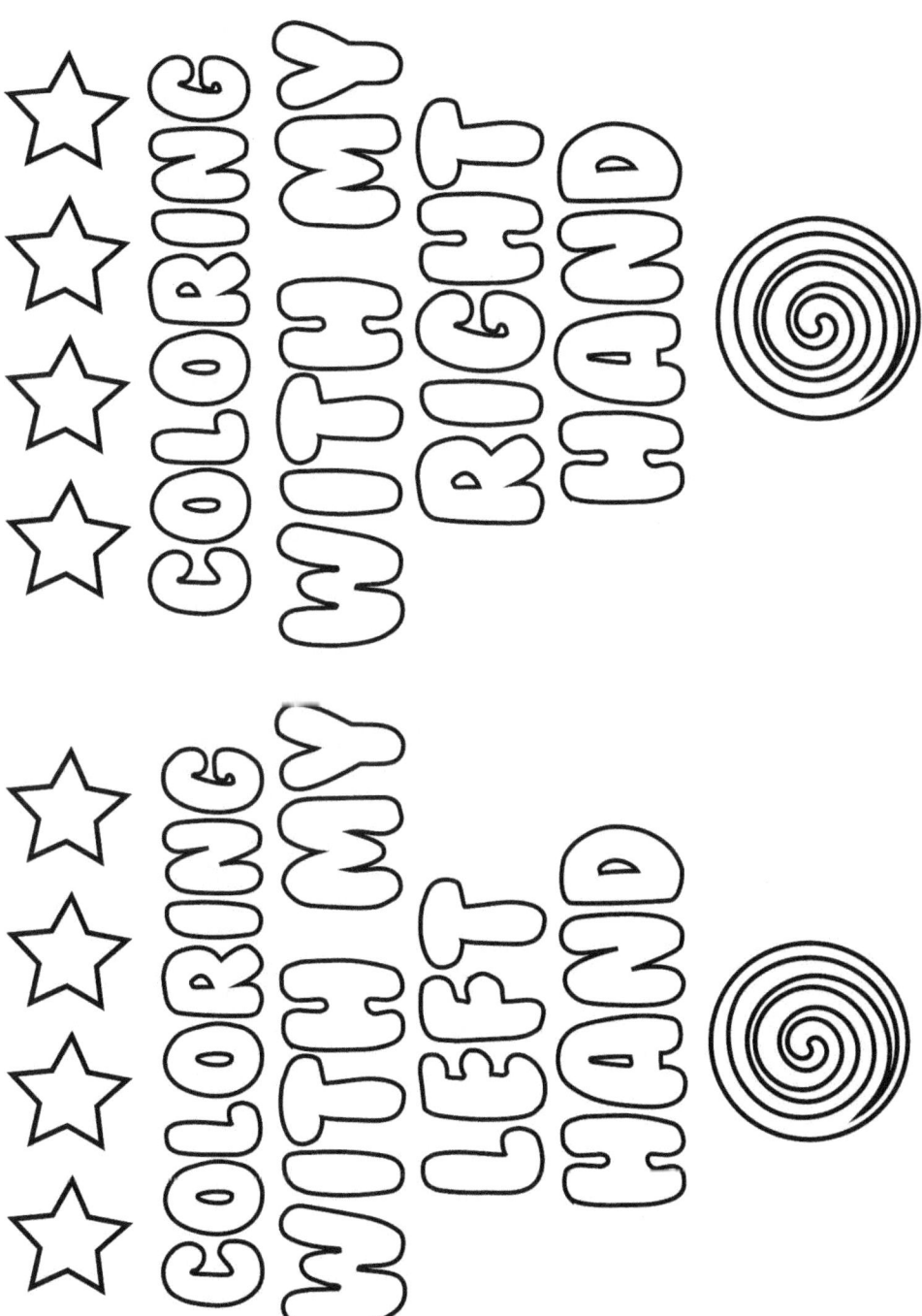

TRUTH

What is your favorite subject in school?

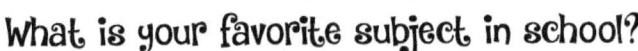

_____

What is your least favorite subject in school?

_____

What is your favorite day of the week?

_____

What is your least favorite day of the week?

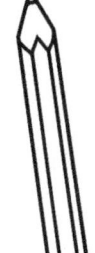

_____

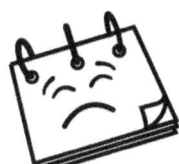

Favorite month of the year?

_____

Least Favorite month of the year?

_____

Favorite time of the day?

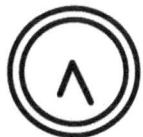

_____

Least favorite time of the day?

_____

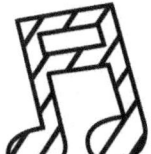

What is your favorite song?

_____

Favorite singer or band?

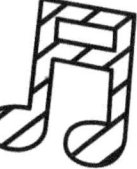

_____

I DARE YOU TO...

COLOR THIS UPSIDE DOWN PICTURE WITHOUT TURNING IT RIGHT SIDE UP!

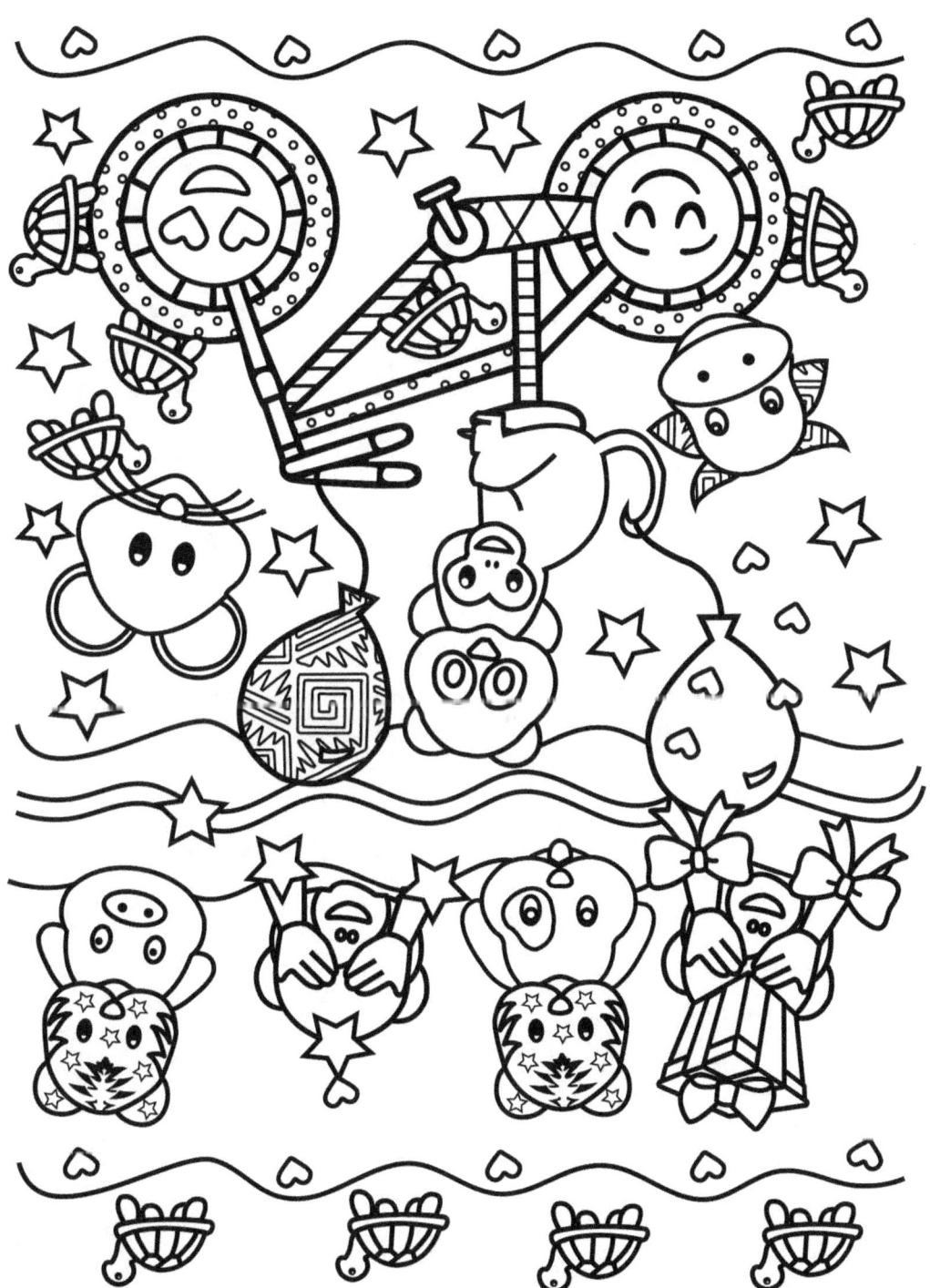

TRUTH
WHAT ARE YOU AFRAID OF?

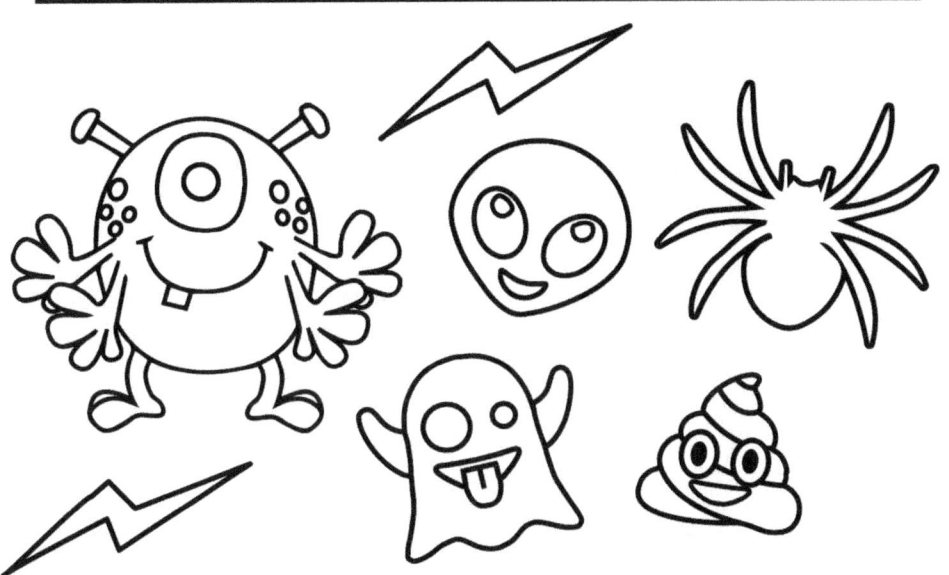

WHAT IS THE SCARIEST THING YOU HAVE EVER DONE?
(draw a picture of it or write about it)

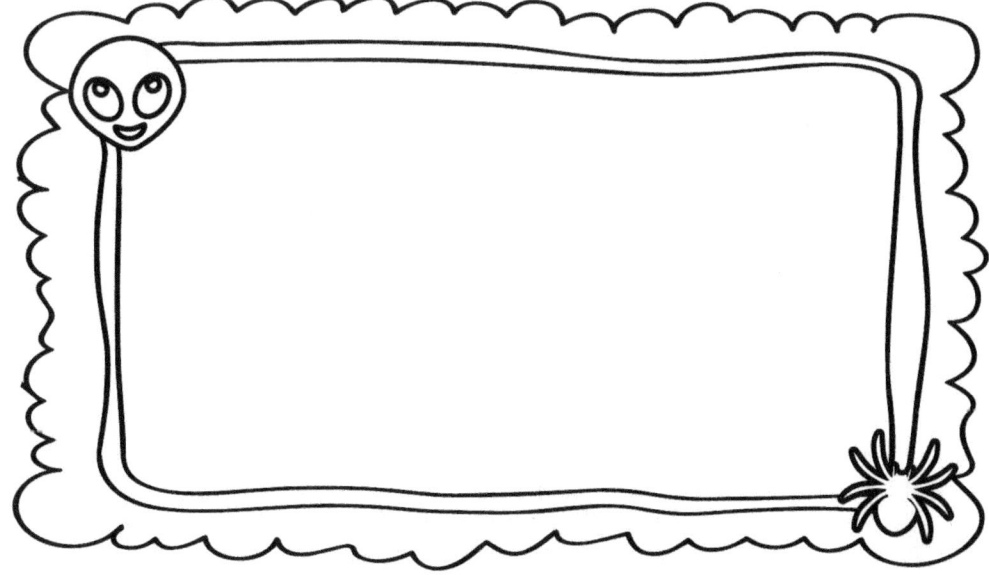

I DARE YOU TO...

COLOR THIS WITHOUT MOVING YOUR HAND. WHAT???
MOVE THE COLORING BOOK BACK AND FORTH TO COLOR !!
THE DESIGNS ARE REPEATED SO YOU CAN PRACTICE.

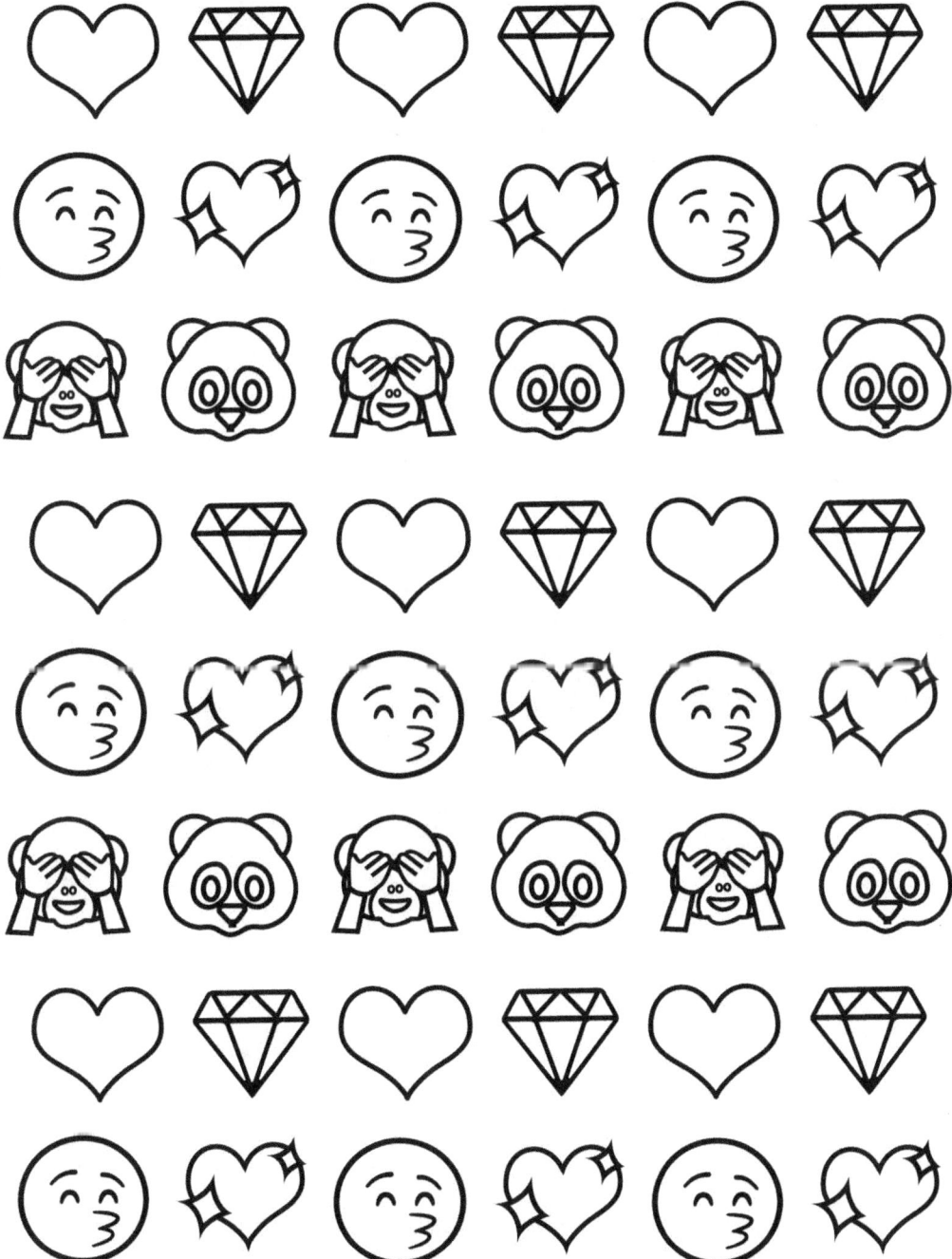

TRUTH

If you could have anything in the world what would it be?

_____

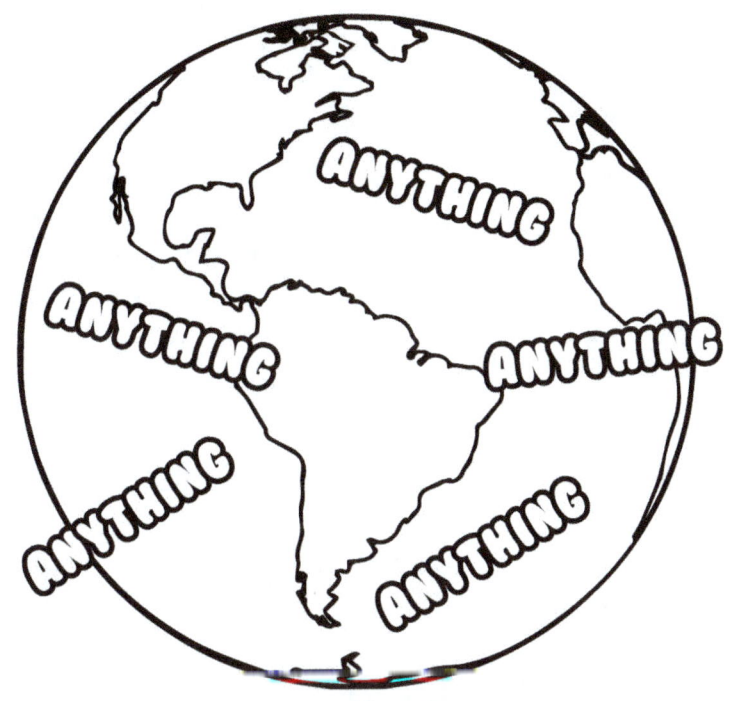

If you could have any super power what would it be?

_____

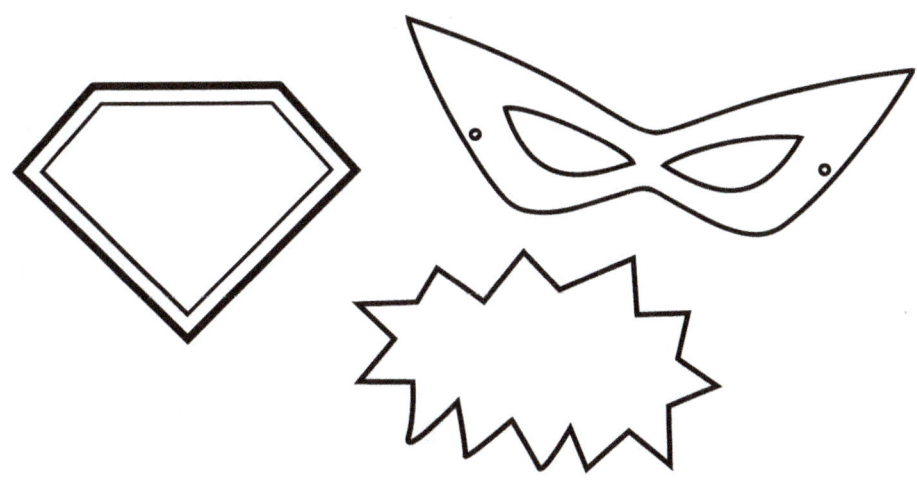

I DARE YOU TO...

COLOR EVERYTHING ON THIS PAGE ONE COLOR. JUST PICK <u>ONE</u> COLOR!

TRUTH

⭐ light ⭐ bright, first ⭐ 👁 see tonight
wish I may wish I might have this wish I wish tonight

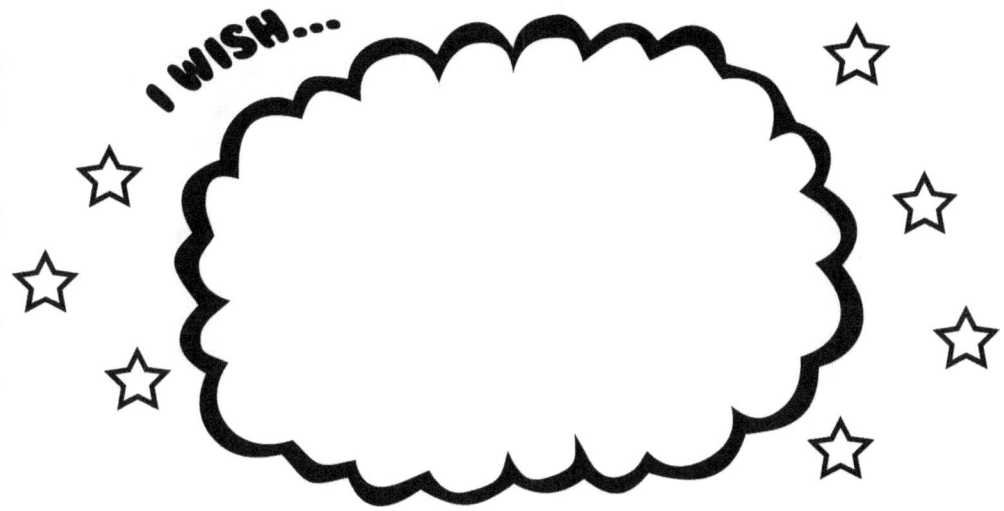

What is the best dream you ever had?

_____

_____

_____

_____

What is your dream job?

_____

_____

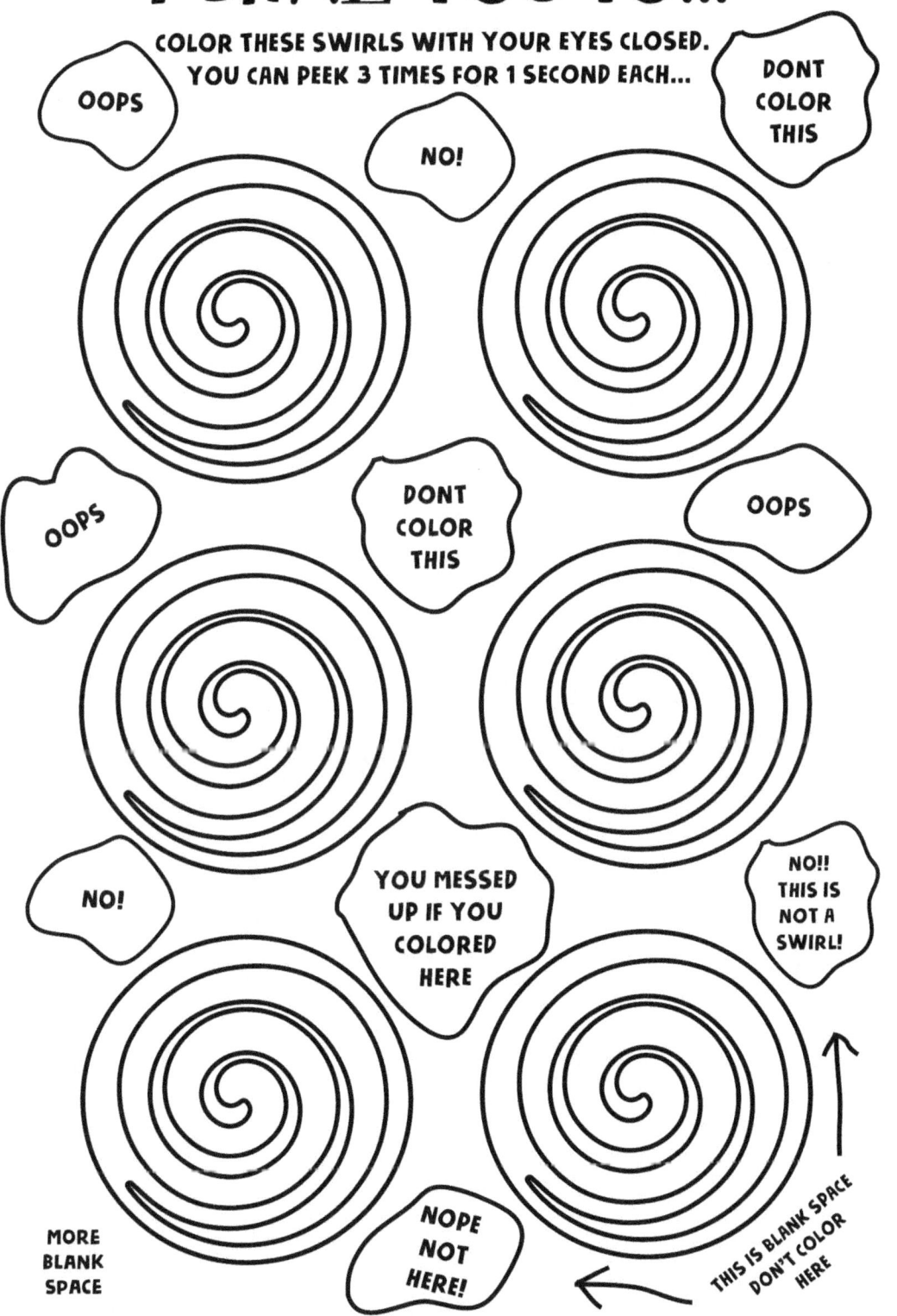

TRUTH

Would you rather live at a carnival or at a zoo? (Color your choice)

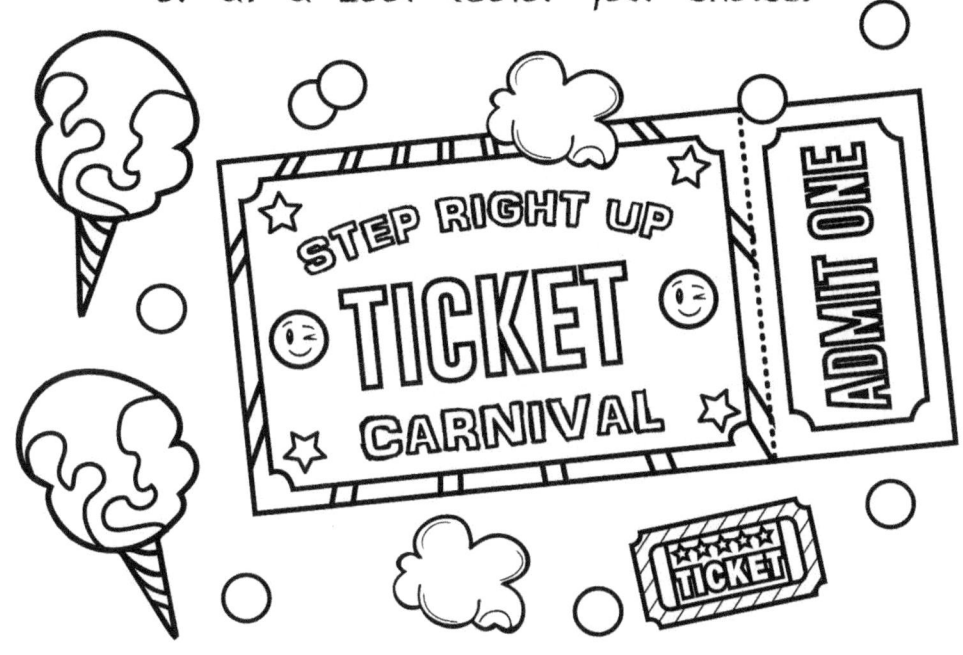

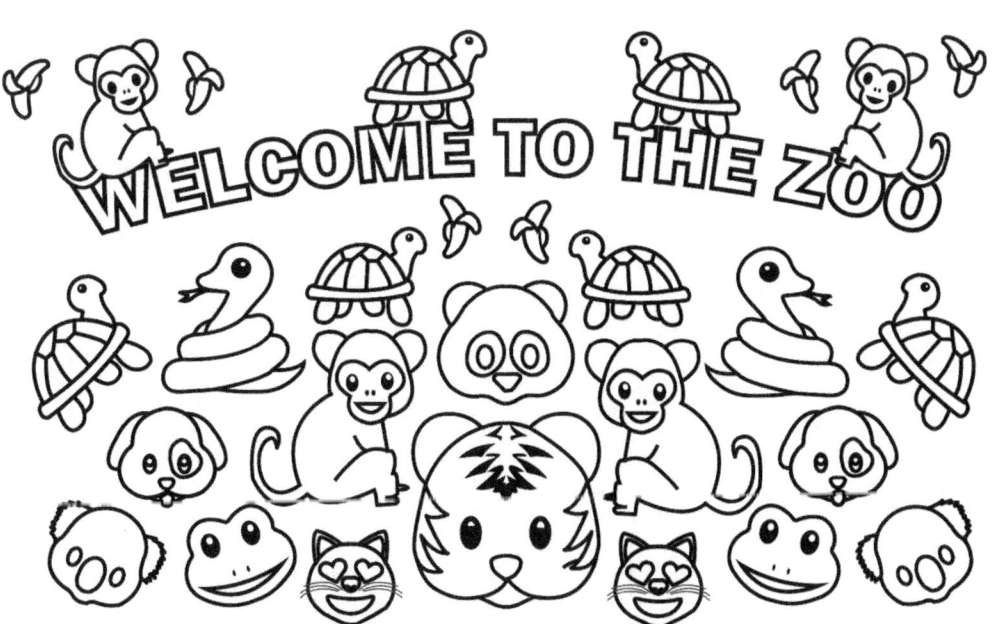

I DARE YOU TO...

COLOR EVERY SHAPE ON THIS PAGE OUTSIDE THE LINES.
DO NOT COLOR ANYTHING NEATLY !

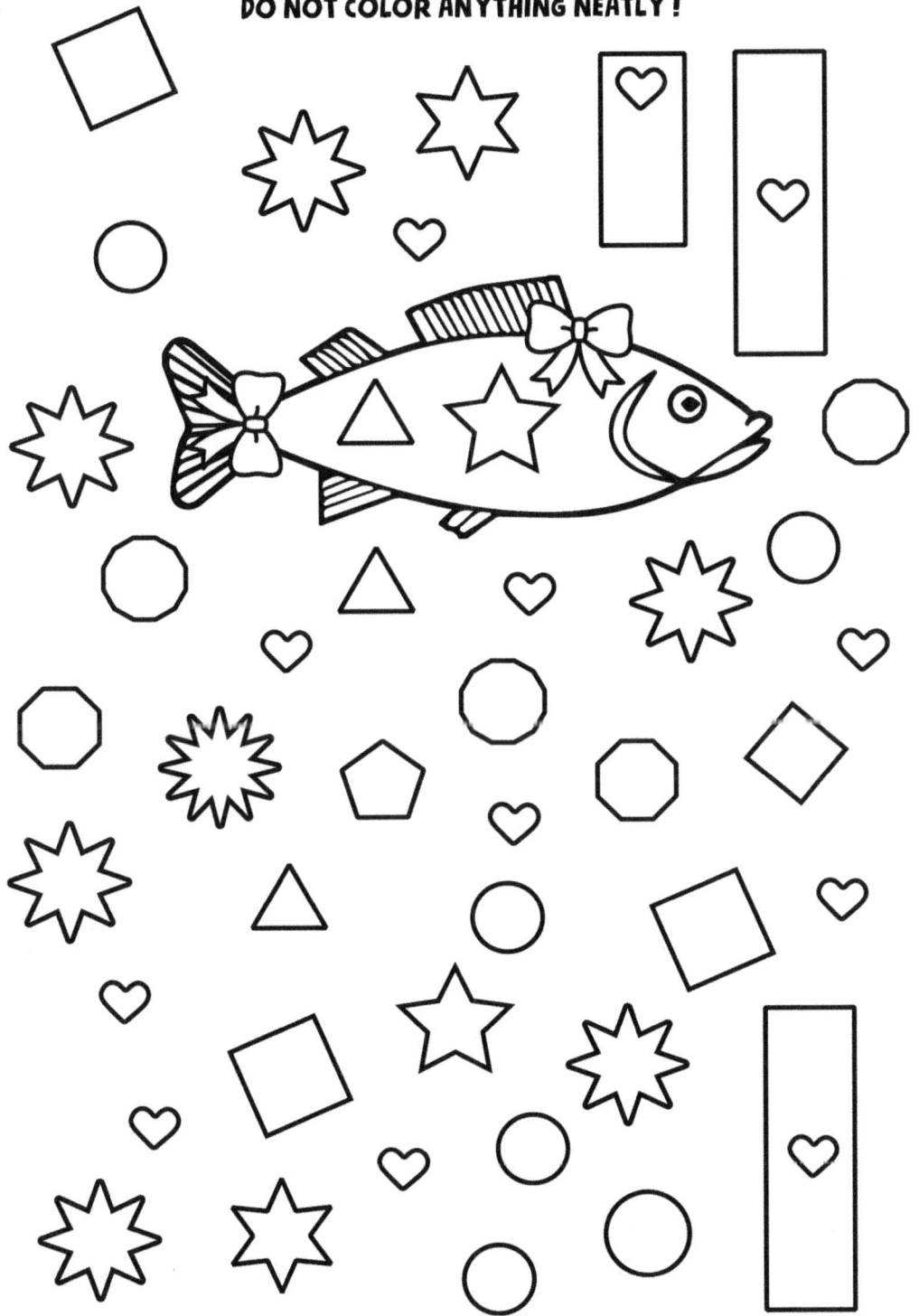

TRUTH

WOULD YOU RATHER...

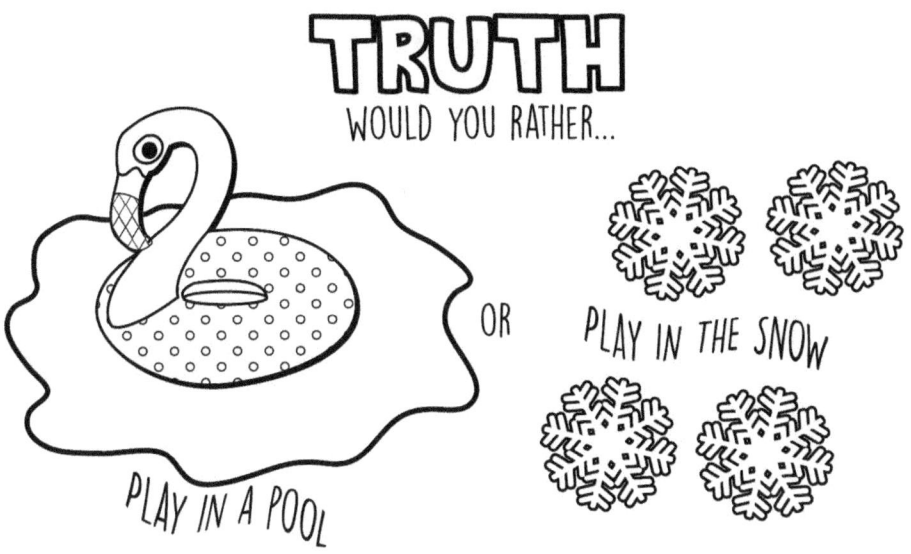

PLAY IN A POOL

OR

PLAY IN THE SNOW

WHAT IS YOUR FAVORITE SUMMER MEMORY?

_____

WHAT'S THE BEST THING ABOUT WINTER?

_____

WOULD YOU RATHER
(Color your answer)

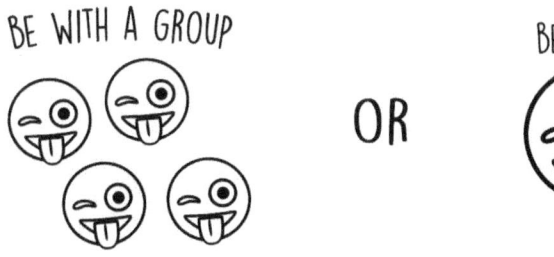

BE WITH A GROUP

OR

BE ALONE

HAVE A CAR THAT CAN

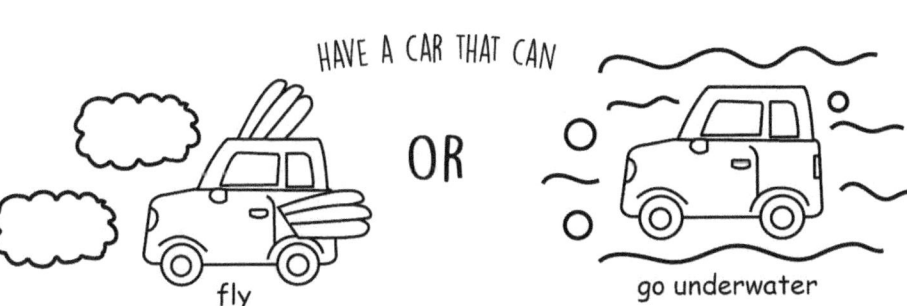

OR

fly

go underwater

I DARE YOU TO...

ONLY COLOR 25 OF THESE POLKA DOTS. I KNOW YOU WANT TO
COLOR THEM ALL, BUT DON'T DO IT!

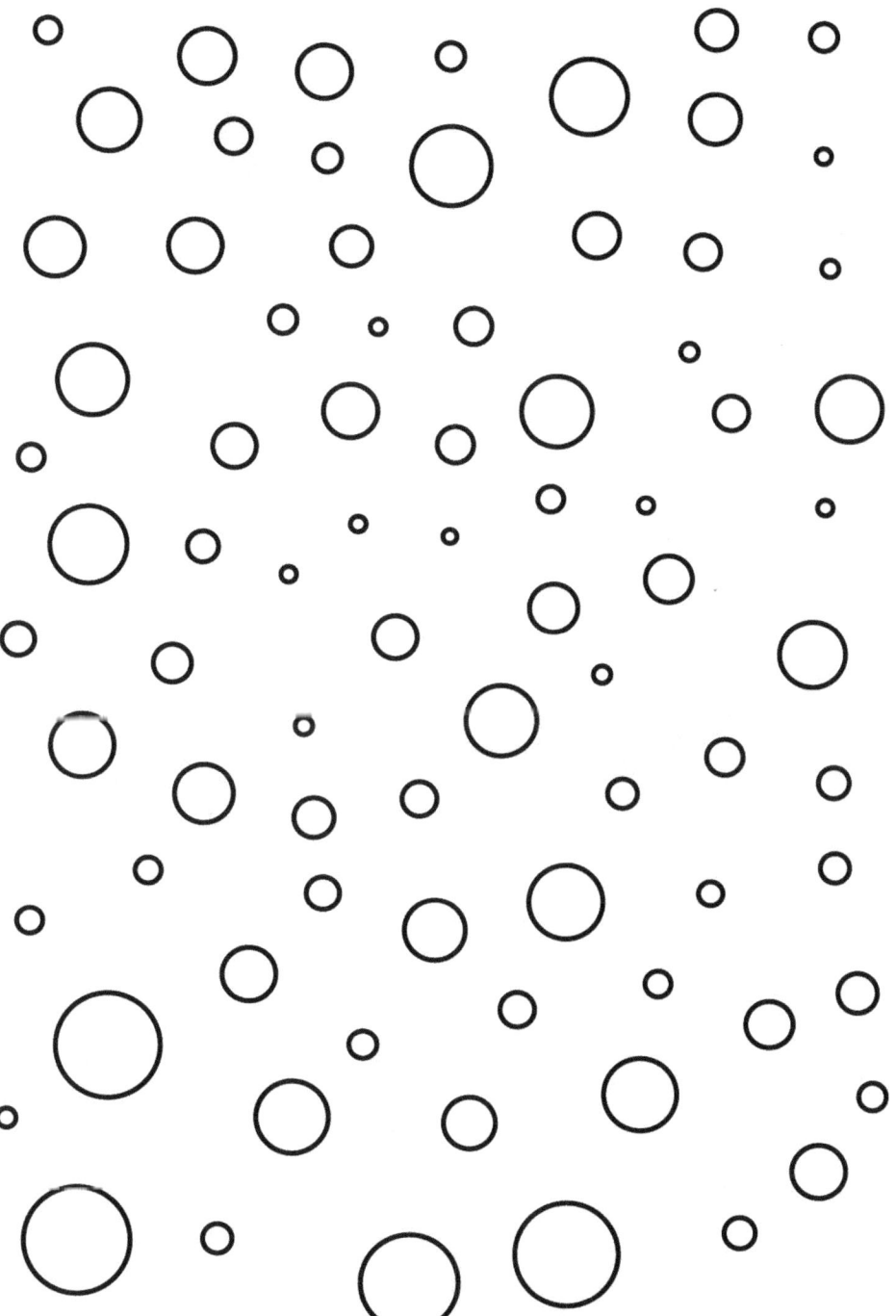

TRUTH

What is best gift you ever received?

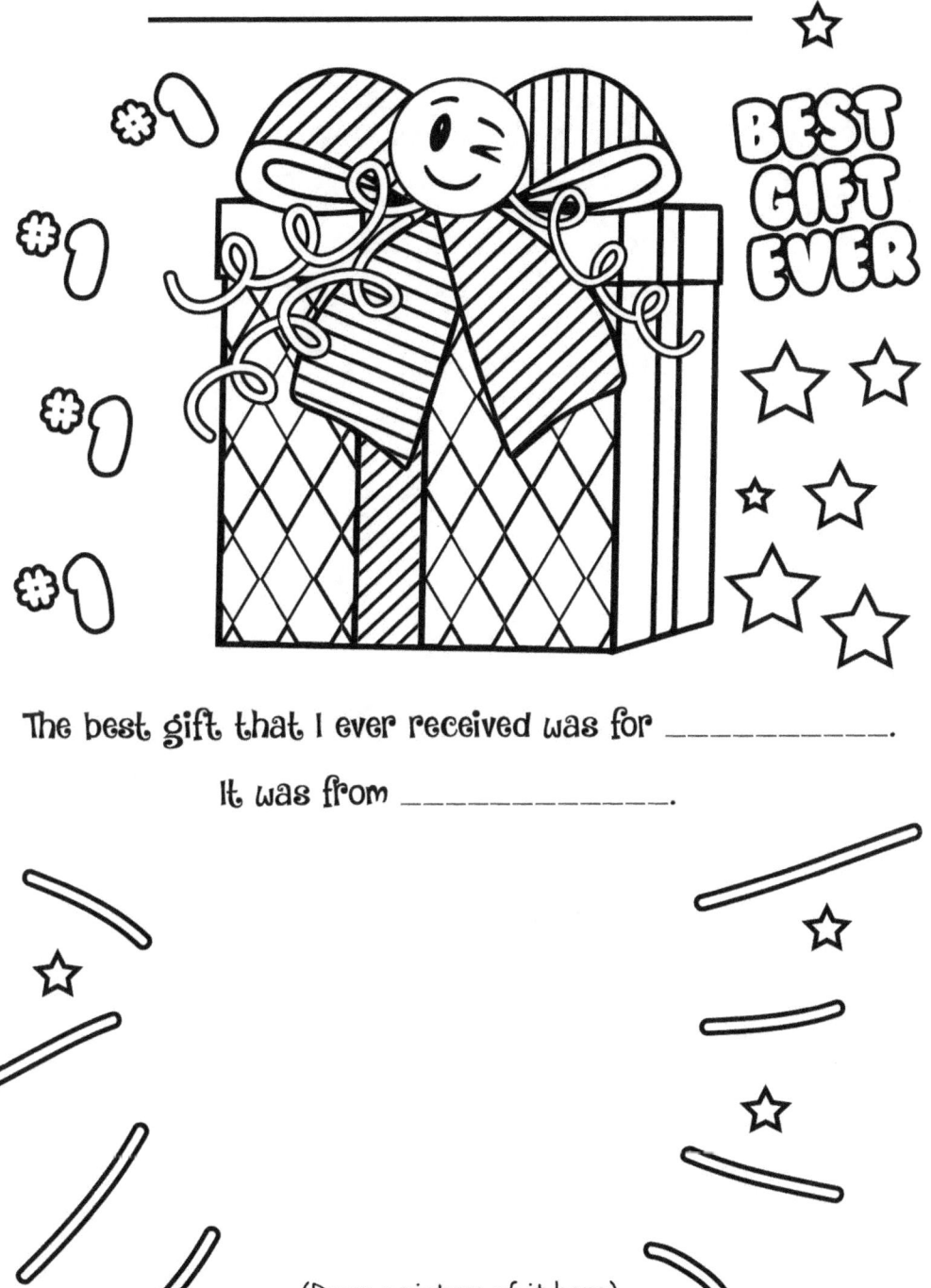

_____

The best gift that I ever received was for _____.

It was from _____.

(Draw a picture of it here)

I DARE YOU TO...

GIVE THIS PUPPY A MOHAWK.
TATTOOS. A NOSE RING. EARRINGS. SPIKES. AND TIE DYE FUR!
AND THEN...COLOR EVERYTHING IN WITH YOUR FOOT

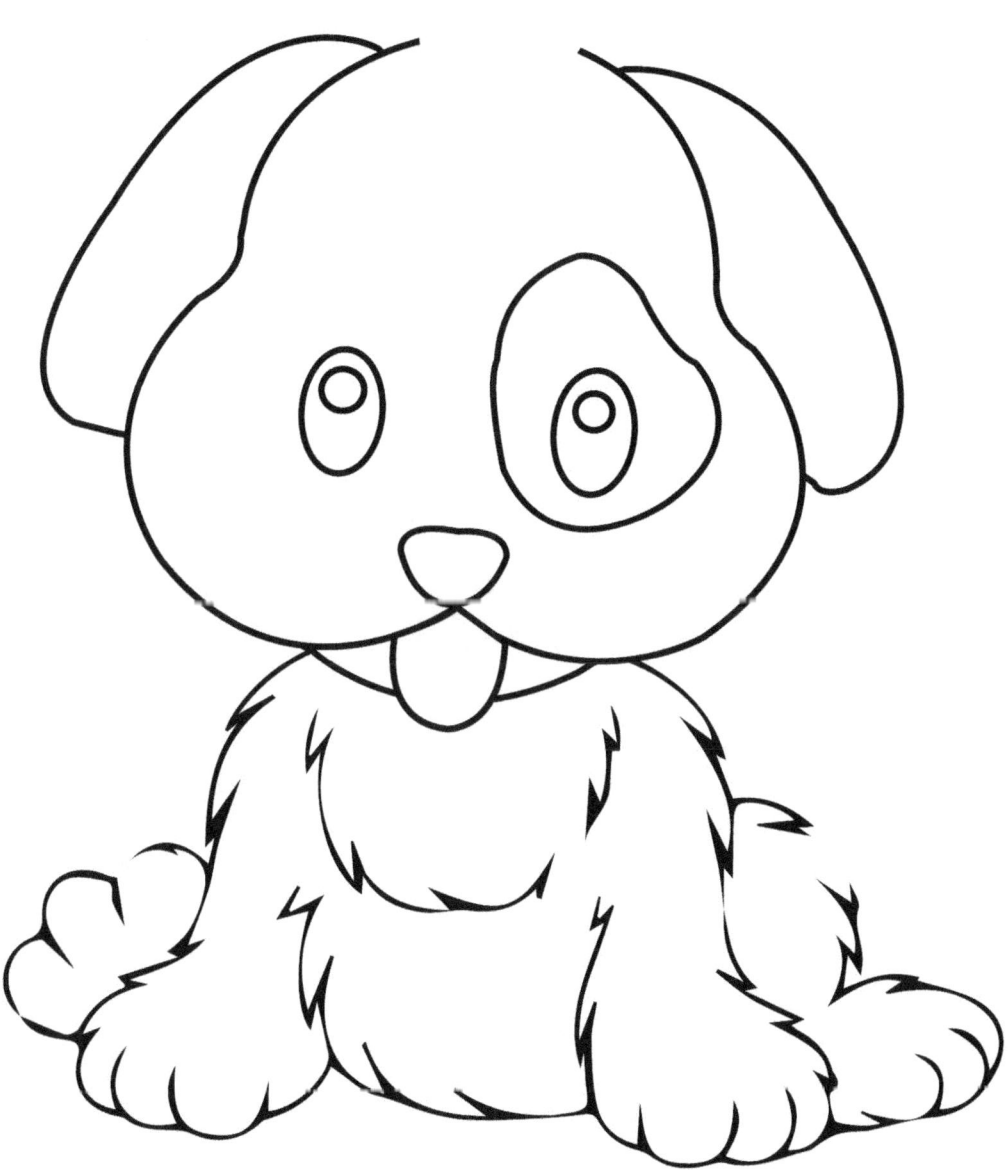

TRUTH

I love to eat _____

I love to drink _____

I love to watch _____

I love to draw _____

I love to play _____

I love to sing _____

I love to go to _____

I love the animal _____

I love the smell of _____

I love the sound of _____

I love this fruit _____

I love this dessert _____

I love this vegetable _____

I love this town _____

I love this country _____

I love this emoji _____

I love this magical creature _____

I love these people _____

_____

_____

I DARE YOU TO...

COLOR EVERYTHING THE WRONG COLOR

WHATEVER YOU DO, DON'T COLOR THE SUN YELLOW, DON'T COLOR THE GRASS GREEN,
DON'T COLOR THE SKY BLUE, DON'T COLOR THE PANDA BLACK AND WHITE...YOU GET IT...

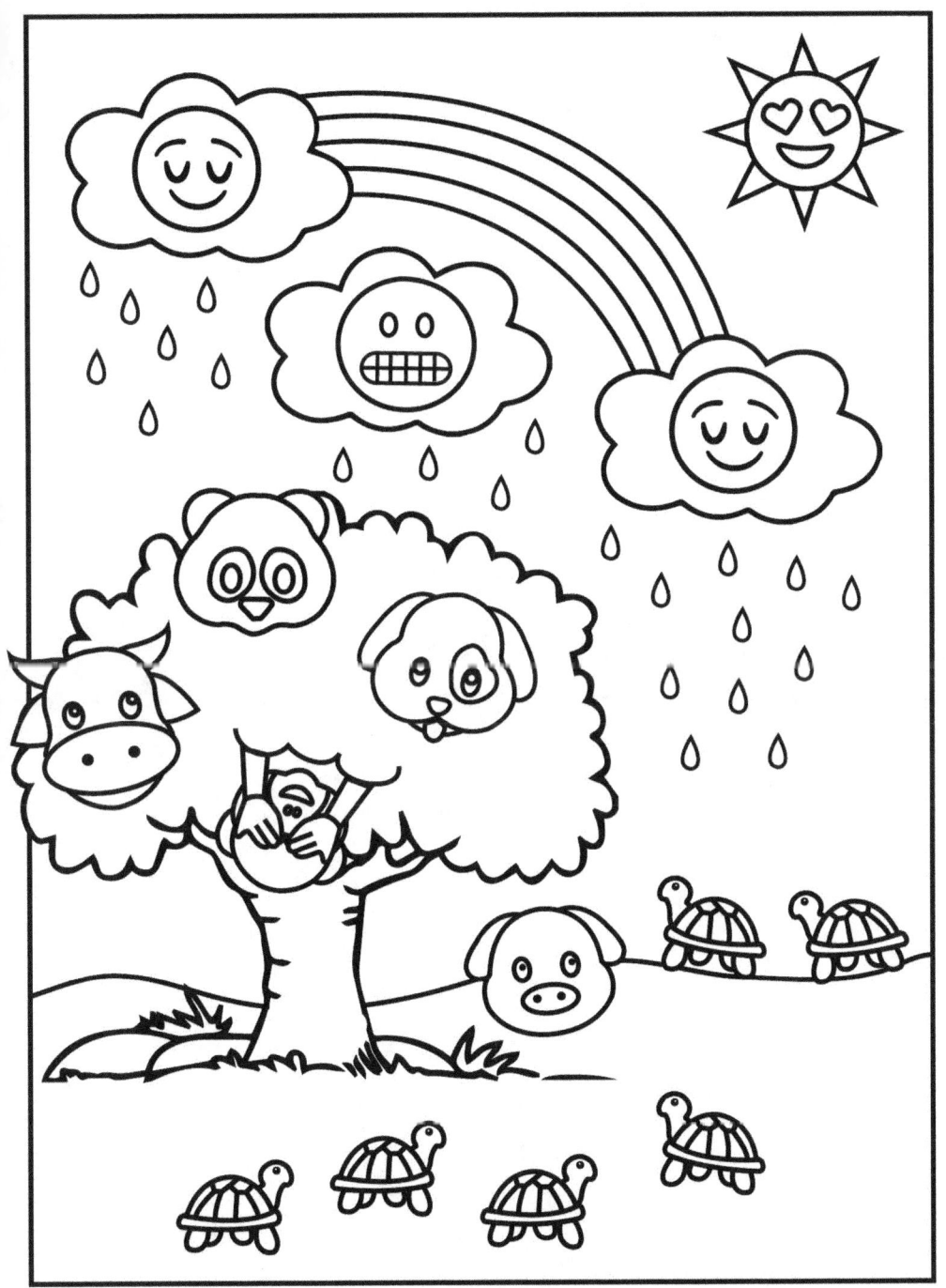

I DARE YOU TO...

DRAW A CUPCAKE WITH YOUR OTHER HAND.
COLOR IT IN WITH YOUR FOOT.

CUPCAKE DRAWN WITH MY _____ HAND.

CUPCAKE COLORED WITH MY _____ FOOT.

TODAY'S DATE: _____

I DARE YOU TO...

DRAW 4 EMOJI FACES WITH YOUR EYES CLOSED.
YOU CAN OPEN THEM TO LOOK WHEN YOU'RE ALL DONE.
THEN CLOSE YOUR EYES AGAIN AND TRY TO COLOR THEM.

MY NAME IS _____ TODAY'S DATE IS _____
I DREW AND COLORED THESE EMOJIS WITH MY EYES CLOSED.
HAHAHAH.

TRUTH

WHAT WAS YOUR FAVORITE TRUTH PAGE IN THIS BOOK?

_____

WHAT WAS YOUR FAVORITE DARE PAGE IN THIS BOOK?

_____

WHICH DARE PAGE WAS THE MOST DIFFICULT?

_____

I DARE YOU TO THINK OF 3 OF YOUR OWN TRUTH QUESTIONS
AND THEN ANSWER THEM...

1. _____

_____

2. _____

_____

3. _____

_____

www.ingramcontent.com/pod-product-compliance
Lightning Source LLC
Chambersburg PA
CBHW071821170526
45167CB00003B/1392